A BETTER WORD
FOR THE WORLD

or

HEAVEN'S
PROXY

or

WATERFALLS

A BETTER WORD FOR THE WORLD

Daniel Bailey

Hannah,

I hope a raccooooooon destroys your enemies tonight.

—Danl Bailey

APOCALYPSE PARTY

A Better Word for the World

ISBN-13: 978-1-7335694-8-4
ISBN-10: 1-7335694-8-0

Cover design by Laura Theobald

www.apocalypse-party.com

Printed in the U.S.A

CONTENTS

THE LIGHTNING ROD OF EVERYTHING

Your phalanx explodes under the launched boulder

We met at a chess tournament for near-nudists
where I wore a single Japanese beetle
and you wore a smear of red dirt

It was the year that we grew a tree
in every room of our dream coffin

We threw bankers off a bridge

You felt you would not let go of the body but you did
It became clear that you were in love with the body
So you erected a flagpole in the hole in a room
in our dream coffin where a tree once stood

You made a flag out of some fabric where our dream coffin lid

The flag tattered as all flags tatter
The tatters were taken down

You spent years making the flag pole into a lightning rod
I had a stroke and you cared for me
You gave me wine enemas nightly
You wired me to the lightning rod of everything
We are waiting for a strike
and have survived many storms

1

TONIGHT YOU WILL LOVE A RIVER

You start a mattress company called Riverbeds

I am one of your first dead
You are one of my first loves

Riverbeds sell especially well to lovers of rivers

It is easy to understand why I have been brought here
when I pace inside my own body
I sell videos of myself pacing inside my own body

I hope to one day buy a riverbed

You realize mosquitos only like a certain part of your body
and you lose sleep trying to think of a way
to get them to love the rest

"You realize what is true about love has been true for so long"
spoken softly over the image of a winding river
moving at the speed of a near-flat earth
would make a good Riverbed commercial, you think
as you enter the covers of your own Riverbed

Tonight you will love a river
or you will love something else

But how the river cannot escape the bed

You love the river
or you love something else

OF FLESH AND BONE

We see a tombstone that is a billboard
that reads "TOO MANY PEOPLE"

I am tired for all the wrong reasons

We see a natural disaster
where all leaves in a forest fall simultaneously

Living is far too marketable
Which natural disaster is the most marketable?

Every natural disaster has been or will be made into a movie
starring Nicolas Cage or Tom Hanks
or a CGI dreamscape will collapse upon us

I want to start manufacturing tombstones out of plastic
My product will be called "Tombplastics"
but everyone will call still call them "tombstones"

"No amount of rain will be able to wash away your name"
will be a line in a Tombplastic commercial

We see a wasp on the ceiling
We see a fruit so big that it rips off the branch on which it grows
We see you entering your closet, becoming a skeleton

I have survived every war that has been fought during my lifetime
When the next one happens you will emerge
in the fabric of your own beauty and collapse

WE BEGIN BY EXPLODING

Everyone on earth is the aftermath of so many explosions
Dead rockets absorbed into the soil of their own inspiration
The universe-shaped womb pendants that bump
gently against our sternums
tell the others what we believe in

After so many gentle sternum bumps
the pendants will detonate
and that is the resolution of our belief

There will be no moment of validation
prior to the point at which
you are spread across the earth as a fertilizer

Your bones are ground and set
into the shape of a tombstone that reads
"Humpty Dumpty is not an egg"

The tombstone is turned on its face and used as a card table
But sometimes it is used as an ironing board
But sometimes you function as a true believer
And you love all of God's creatures out of a sense
of obligation to the logic that love heals all wounds
and unites the universe with the way that you perceive it

That your love is so often denied is immaterial
that you drape across your face as you weep

THE UNPLANNED UPON MORNING

Rarely does nothing become

It is silly to grapple with meaning
when what is real is so obvious

The bobsled full of hot wings glides
slow across the ice before taking flight

It is because there is a volcano below you
that you must bury the reed in your lungs

and God must know that there will never again be a time
But you are made, something will reply
You hear a baby babble that this is all against its will
And so the baby will wake up and wake up
It will wake up into your crying arms

There is a joy I have yet to live, I tell myself
That is my morning - it is my commute

I feel tethered to the powerlines
Like a child to a zip line
I have grown old thinking of this
I must rejoice that I have grown

THE BIG BANG REACHES THE SHORE

It's funny how kids these days
don't go ding-dong ditching death's ding-a-ling
Back when I was but a tadpole
sucking on the kneehole
high above the pond
it was a doorstep that led to the door
and not the other way around
And instead of a white light it was a party
and death and the just dead all kicked back into life
And life was not a thing that you wanted
You wanted the step beyond the door
and to see what was beyond that first step
How you would follow your own de-evolution up the stairs
First the man erect
Then the man slouched then the ape
Then the tadpole
Then the mud
Then the water and the dirt separately alone
And sometimes you feel like a dot
and sometimes you don't

YOUR SILLINESS IS TOO MUCH FOR LIFE

The song is the polar opposite of life
Which is not death but a cluster of all possibility
that you drag behind your body
like cans after a marriage

But how pleasing it is to be folded into the rug
scream the dust mites of my soul

You will go unnoticed
and into the palewood floor
We will all be lost again
We will view one another as trees
all of us lost in the forest of other lives

We must all write our young adult novel
or every second your punk band dies

But graduate deep into the cricket heap
But wait for a new stage of grief

But you are in it

But now you order a bumper sticker that reads
"In memory of [my son] 1998-2016" and never rip the envelope
it arrives in

And I am just too fucking happy to be cast into a statue
And the firewood make a good house
And someone is already logged into your machine

YOU WILL LIVE A DREAM-FREE LIFE

Your drone will fall in love with someone else's drone

You will enter your bed and you will cease to exist
for however many hours your spirit will allow
and then the next day your life will be spirit-free

You will break every bone in your body
by the tender hum of your love
You had learned to resist your own longing
to turn it inward

Your tombstone will be a glass hummingbird
that spews sugar water from its tiny beak
using the same technology as pissing boy fountains

Deprived children will drink the sugar water
and they will hum through the cemetery's leafless canopy

Your love has left contrails

It's been so long since they called anything sin
Ah but when will love catch up with me, you seem to exude

But they are already working on it
In fact, they are at war

11

YOU LIGHT THE CITRONELLA

A day after spraying the backyard with pesticides
we discover the corpses of insects we never knew existed

That same day you watch a student perform
a Bing image search for "holocaust gas chambers"
which produces pictures of empty concrete rooms
"I bet that shit haunted as fuck," he says

We wait for a moment when it is ok to celebrate
but we can't wait
We are drunk all the time, regardless
Why else would we let the trees grow so crooked?

We are careful not to apply too much caution to any situation
You break your toe beneath the shutting door
You must explain your brokenness to the world
I give you a hug after receiving an electric shock from the water heater

By the time we celebrate the electricity is already gone

We have been celebrating for years
We love to celebrate with our city, which is new to us
We are learning to celebrate as they celebrate
You light the citronella
let the mosquitoes fight the flame to feast

BELOW THE HOVERING ID

A bug too small to identify crawls around on the screen
You feel confident that blowing it off will do it no harm
You like these nights where you can smell yourself
That's how invested your body is in its own experience
but also how much the graveyard of your experience
must keep the silliest flowers at dead hand always
Though impermanence is in love or more like has a crush
that you will share when readiness has gone
to the infinite moon's territory of its own self-orbit
or into the searchlight of your neighborhood's police chopper
where you will be easily id'd as just
who you have always known
pressed firmly into the belief
that you are wrong
which you are not

MY ENTHUSIASTIC RAINSTORM EXTENDS ALSO TO YOU

Mall fountains from your heart
Space mountain runoff feeds the river
Copper from old pennies blossoms in the pool
Algae as green as how the hill volcanoed

———————

I try to climb the kudzu
It seems to break before I can stand
The power lines unzip over the hills

———————

A grandma gripes the god that shows
the severed stinger its gone bee host
the middle finger of the ghost
to god in a state of ripe

—I hope at some point in my life to plant the garden I meant for
tomorrow—

The dead tree leafless above us
(Cristo Redentor without a shirt)
To drink both the water and wine

The Payless Shoe store to be, one day
hosted in my memorial strip mall's feet

———————————————

There is ultimately nothing to say
To be my own finished thought chopped like dust
in the ceiling fan or just blessed
to be handling my own caterwauling pulse
and not the taunting want of what all else

"SHORTAGE" VS. "SCARCITY"

Everyone keeps saying it's just common sense
but it takes a lot to be of little use

I watch my own use move like a tide

Just today I handed someone a dictionary
He had asked me the difference between "shortage" and "scarcity"
The dictionary was my attempt to say I did not know
but that I hope to discover the difference with you

I describe how I wake up to my pillow
and my pillow cannot deny my description
because it is not alive
or it does not have the ability to communicate
the way that I do

The beauty of being misunderstood

The sharpening of how I communicate

That the perfect metaphor for now
would be trying to explain metaphor
without an example in mind

Or at least in the part of my mind that my moment can reach

That "seeing the forest for the trees" means
you are able to stand at the edge of a forest
and trust that beyond your own line of vision into the forest
that yes there are more trees still
and not simply a wall painted
to create the illusion of more trees

I have fought with that wall
I have thought time and again thought time
Thought there is nothing more than this
and there need be nothing more than this

PRELUDE TO LOVE COUNTRY

Over the hill somewhere is an empty field
where they are playing the audio of riots
letting it swell
Then pausing the audio
                          turning the volume knob left
Letting it swell
                          turning the volume knob left
It is the way the cicadas wake up
          you don't even notice it
Until the swell exhumes you too
and then it is gone
You think to ride the Atlanta Highway
to see where it ends up
You wonder how often it misses its target
Then the audio of a laser is played in an empty field somewhere
maybe somewhere beyond the next hill
The riot continues to swell
The dead feel so proud of the living
And the living feel so proud of the dead
Between the riot swells we picnic
You say, there is love in this place
I say, I know

ORB-WEAVER

A spider between two pillars
making its web a foreground to dusk's cracking

I called to you and you arrived
I said get the camera
and you got the camera
and you flashed the web
like lightning through a cloud

The spider did not react
it kept building its web
in the glow
the anti-shadow of the earth
the weaver kept pulling threads from its self
placing them where they needed to be
and I thought about fishing lures
and so many fish
it costs a lot to live
and I'm learning to love that
to love horribly
to lick silence like a web
let the taste of paper fill my mouth

THE TREES VIBRATE WILDLY

I try to imagine a lack of atmosphere
I look at you looking at the trees
and you do not look back
and I enjoy that you do not look back
We decide to go inside
and I don't know
something

We probably have a beer and I play pool
while you sit at the computer and work
or we watch the Aviator starring Leo D
and my feet touch your feet
and our bodies are still
while the trees vibrate wildly
Our bodies the strangest planets
our lungs containing breath
that when lit will explode

JOY YOUR HEART AGAINST ME

I screech against the windy parts of me
I unsing little by little
witness pays its own bills like a boyfriend
without feelings I am a perfect person
with feelings I am just another person
my joy needs to be stamped
on the heart of the nation it belongs to
someone put me on a bus
headed toward some central location
I want to take the bus hostage
like Dennis Hopper in Speed
and joyride around doing 50+
I pet dogs I pet dogs I pet dogs
wear suns wear lakes wear dreams
dream like I have dreamed of late
of a church where everyone
tries to kill me
as a form of worship
every part of me ready
to be held underwater

HALO

The fan chain ticking against the bulb
made me want the light to break
upon me like a shivering mess of data
that my skin could not possibly compute or reconcile
I have watched dudes shoot people online
and enjoyed the feeling I get from bones
wading softly against my legs off the dock
I want to stare into a screen some more
I want a character from the game to pull me
into the game
like that A-Ha video but with bloody battle
where I shoot and get shot and return
to a place I have never been
somewhere in Iraq or Poland
and I get up and walk around pointing my gun
and I get shot again
and it happens again
and again
and I walk to the water
where I am shot once again
and I am regenerated
but now I am a minnow
and a turtle snatches me
and now I am the water
and you drink me

WE DON'T DIE / WE MULTIPLY

I had a religious experience walking through Wal-Mart
My two-hour wait at the Tire and Lube let
the store move me through its aisles
taking photos of the dying fish and plastic bouquets

I followed a family into the Garden Center
and watched employees
take it apart for a new season
How I wish I could be
taken apart with every season
How I should be cleaned
and stuffed with every Christmas bulb

and Lately I am growing blanker and blanker
I have drunk the inside of a helicopter's sky
I will never talk to anyone
ever again I think all
too often that I have doomed myself
to a glut of not feeling

or how I could possibly be of use without you
and how could I possibly be of use without every one of you

OVERWHELMED

I throw my dog off the splintered dock
and follow her into the lake
swim to where my feet can scratch the red clay
and pull it toward the surface
where it is raining
not because it is August
but because this is the kind of thing
that happens in August

I let my palm rest beneath the quivering surface
try to feel how far down
a raindrop can penetrate a lake
I find it impossible to identify
the variables of here or now
or the faulty triggers
of my past hope left useless

by decision or by the bleak fortune
that we have named Outcome
My dog is so terrified to swim
and I am so eager to force her
to be so constantly overwhelmed
that it becomes nothing
or so like nothing
that I mistake the scratch marks
from the dog's frantic paddling

for the red Georgia clay
attaching itself to my skin
to remind me of where I am
and who I am in it

SHAKY HANDS

I put my dog out in the rain
so she can stare at trees
and I can enjoy being alone
with music and beer
and then turn the music off
and then finish the beer
It's like I am a splinter
off a fallen branch
beneath wet leaves

and I walk through me
or against a tide
so thick with life
that it stings to try
to follow a raindrop
to the core of the earth
or like when I check the wifi
or make sure I capitalize the right letters
to know that I will not be
left with the old news of you

Throw a funeral against the screen
and watch it crack
like a branch in heavy weather
in whatever month it is
in whatever home I inhabit

for whatever time this is
and if time means wriggle I wriggle
and if dance then dance

and if burn then burn beneath the leaves
to the color of leaves
in whatever time of year it is

YOU BEAUTIFUL RIVER YOU

I want to make you a river
and float down you on a raft of you too
and caterwaul over your cliffs
and break at your lower waters
and feel those waters sting my eyes
and crush my sinuses
and let my face touch the riverbed
and when I surface float face down
and feel my skull knock against a rock repeatedly
        but gently like a restless leg under a table
and I want to sit on all the rocks on earth
        for at least several moments apiece
        even the tiny ones
and let each rock pass its pulse onto me
and let me kiss each rock on the mouth
and breathe its breath and try hard
        to remember the breath that I am given
        that I cannot count the clouds on a beautiful day
        that the air is not a filter for light
        that light like light
        will cloud your waters
        that I will let stones sink
        like dropped harps
        or float like pianos
        midstream

CASUALTIES

I cannot even walk through the woods
without walking through a spider web or
catching eight caterpillars on my tee shirt
or looking down for a new body
or not finding a new body
looking up at me

I cannot not cry now that I think of it

Two mushrooms geysering blood
and all of us dancing

We've just been hired as astronauts
I am up in space
I will damage the controls and strand myself up here
and I will look at the earth and weep
and I will weep
I will weep

and I will put on my deathsuit
and cancel my Netflix
and I will wade through the revisions of my life
and I will weep
or I will weep and give a speech
and I will drive a nail through my mouth
and my mouth will weep

O let every river fill me

with whatever water is searching

for I am the future bloated

a self scraping against a reef

or a kitchen sponge that has hardened

during the course of a vacation

SKYMALL

We have ordered our tombstones and deathrings
33,000 feet above a part of Iowa
that has been mapped and then forgotten

You discover that love
like all activities
must be put to rest occasionally

It seems tragic to discover this

You cope by buying comfort items for your dog
whose occasions of love come more frequently
perhaps, you think
in a manner that reflects
the dog's shorter life span
which also intensifies your own need
to express love

There is not a voice you would trust to express
the way god feels for you
which you are still avoiding

I love the idea that the sky is a wall
with a hidden door
and that behind that door
is more sky

How sweet it is to watch two dogs
drink simultaneously from the same water
only moments after play-killing one another

Or how it's possible that your biological life span
simply does not coincide
with one of god's fierce bouts of love for you

Or the dogmatic sensibilities through which
we all must discover the tame logic of acceptance

Try asking a loved one what they would
if you left them, without notice, tomorrow

It is impossible

But then you are asked, late spring
to lie beneath a deciduous and blow
every one of its leaves off
with your breath

And you misinterpret the directions to mean
"lie face down and blow into the earth"
as if the earth needs your input

But we are not buried face down
if we can help it

We draft documents to tell people
to tend to our bodies like a garden or a candle

as if our loves are not sick of the tending

Exhausted from all the moments of love

You buy rings in the air

There is a holocaust beneath you
Or you imagine there to be a holocaust beneath you

You breathe the expired air of they who must sit next to you

You must fear flying at least a little
Hello weapons of humanity, I am human
we seem to think as one

But it is not enough to be human - I am up here like a tree
or a heaven uprooted

Somewhere the blast of time against all time
Or the calm, hollow attitude I hope to one day stuff
with lit firecrackers and magnolias

And to then collect the shrapnel and glass
and be full again with what we have lost

But we sense though we do not know
how much we would miss the idea that our carcasses
will rise and one day, be exposed
our bones the contrails of what we mistake for love

MONUMENT

You specify in your last will and testament
to "bury me where I stand"
so they remove a chunk of tiles from the floor
in front of the Golden Pantry's checkout counter
and they set your feet and the bottoms of your shins
in the dirt below

The rest of you snaps and is removed

The tiles are replaced after the stumps are shortened

It is light wind season, swaying tree season

Somewhere someone
is watching the surveillance footage of your life
trying to find the moment where
we drop an egg in the pan
and it sticks and blossoms and burns
and cannot be scraped off

You begin to feel that adulthood must precede childhood

I arrive to meet you
but the manager of the Golden Pantry
has already replaced the tiles

I check the dumpster out back but you are not there
I check the woods behind the dumpster
I crawl through many obstacles: nettle and briars and barbed wires

I find a neighborhood which I enter through a backyard
nearly tripping on a dog's chain, nearly falling
into a covered pool's puddle in which mosquitoes breed

The mosquitoes believe that life is infinite
and so they sail as near to the sun as they can manage
before returning

They return to make holes in us
and to make new mosquitoes as if to make new clouds

They return to make holes in us

Late one night you ask me
"Do you think mosquitoes make holes that they love?
Holes that they hope to one day return to?"

I fondly remember nightlights   especially when sick

I move beyond the pool
and between two houses
to a foreground to how
people have become hidden

I feel you must be near though I know you are not

I tap my cell phone in the street to see where I am

I am never lost
I set the directions to walk home
until I know where I am
and I am steered away from the bramble and the briar

I pass a woman walking a dog

We claim our sides of the street and say hello

She says nice night   I say I know

You say ok   and the world says I know

They say mosquitoes will eat you alive
You say that's ok they need me alive

THE WATERFALLNESS OF THE WATER

You look down to find the mosquito still attached to your foot
It has died and is now stuck there
You call your spiritual advisor to ask for advice

You feel water opening umbrellas in your cells

Someone says, "I've witnessed so much change in my life
that I wish I could just throw it all in the tip bucket
and be just a little of what I was before now"

Someone else describes how the stars or moon will appear tonight
and tells us when we will see the next meteor shower
and in what part of the sky

At times it seems as though we have already met these challenges
and at other times we are at home walking from one room to the next
trying to imagine our way into the extra room
that we know must be there we have dreamt it
and we only woke up because we crashed our dream family
into the hill nuked with fireflies

Is it inappropriate to feel that we deserve something from life?

I struggle with this all the time

Though maybe the point of life is to eat shit and grow

I still believe in the nuclear family's ability
to eat shit and grow beyond what I alone am capable of

To feel extinct is to carry a little waterfall in half your cells
and a little umbrella in the cells beneath

To say "we're all naked under our clothes"
when we really mean
"under our consciousness the unconscious
under that nothing"

To be interred, I recommend presenting your body
to the earth as a leaf that has fallen, your mouth
inhaling the wetness of dirt between grass and grass
and keeping very still for as long as still can be so very kept

"I'll know it when I see it," says the love and death situation into
its mineshaft

Tonight we watched bats fly about the neighborhood

And yes it is inappropriate to feel
that we deserve something
because who has anything to give
but the present space of time that we now inhabit

I am a body propelled upstream
I knock against rocks and rejoice in the muted percussion

Someone somewhere does something which is how much it seems

There is a new bladder attached to the sky and leaking
The bats around the neighborhood swooped and seemed to enjoy
their flight

It sucks how much of a vapor you try to become

You say you would drink your weight
but really you are only tired enough
to become shitty against your own light

Your spiritual advisor decides that it's all you man you get it girl

That's just how it is
You pull the dead mosquito from your foot
and a tiny stream of blood finds a path against your skin
It follows the inverted riverbed
created by the vessels lifting the roof of your skin

You worry about yourself
and everyone else
and you wonder if this is fair to yourself

Life kills you as life must

You are not that fond of opening your cells
but here you are with all your cells open
like the underside of an umbrella
and it is raining into you

You know the song before it even plays
You ride up to the sun instead of into it
You stare into the sun like a patch of drywall
You dig up the hill and find the statue of its name
We ride down the hill it is bearded with tinder
The hill flattens and the beard burns
against the ever-rising river of ever-rising suns
The face keeps flooding when you realize this
You want to thank God but you don't

We water our bodies unless we forget
I drink the part of a river that moves too fast for disease
You wish to be the thing that was
You are attracted to the doneness
The waterfallness of the water
The illusion of intention in the final thought

RAVEN ROCK CLIFFS

We observe the rock formation from within
while simultaneously finding it impossible
to consider ourselves apart from the instance
of light on the disturbed river

You become interested in what they do
with the defective pieces of artificial hearts, specifically
whether or not they can be used in a different part
of the artificial body

You grew up with the idea that "someday" represented
the possibility of tomorrow and in that tense
you grew into a fit of rapids far deadlier
than the stillness you now seek

That "represented" must in the meanwhile seek to represent

To throw a rock into a river
means to give a piece of the riverbed back
to that which has loosed it from its point of origin

That the one that oversaw your birth
will not be the one to unplug your machine

You climb into the hollow of a rock
I've always known that I can be just like the rafter

stuck in the rapid, body churned until their pieces
were small enough to join the riverbed

There is also the hope to never be found

Hope will someday collide with the continuation of hope

You find yourself surrounded by everyone you love
They have been pounded into dust by a force
that has also revealed your own inner dust

Each speck of mica reveals a tiny detail
about the main idea: that the universe is falling apart
but it is also reassembling at such a slow pace
that we become drunk against our own participation in this cycle

I swallow the starlight while wading up to my knees
I kick up the riverbed so that my feet will disappear

You learn that the cliff above you
is supposedly where Burt Reynolds was filmed
drawing back his arrow in Deliverance
and how that image becomes the gargoyle on the chapel
of the falling apart/reassembly

You imagine a hotel in France where they serve duck into the night
They will deliver a cooked duck to your bed
You imagine a duck landing on the riverbed before you
A business plan is hatched

You will do nothing because the world is currently falling apart

When reassembly begins you will collide with hope
and the collision will nearly kill you

Life will multiply as you aid the reassembly
of the world, you savior you

You will find goats on roofs
Sports will be played in darkness

Your entire life will seem the river on pause
and you will swim upstream
toward what you seem to remember as true

When you describe your business plan to investors
you will be turned down

They will say, what if instead we disassembled
our own bodies or developed a product
to instantaneously disassemble the human body

You will say, yes
but we cannot market time
and time is a thing that everyone already wishes would stop

You leave the meeting an hour later, drenched
from the sprinklers in the ceiling that simulate
downpour on days when rain seems necessary

To make the inside and outside as one again

The street's pavement glints in the sun
and you follow the glow through the forest roads

You cannot find a good place to crash your car
so you walk to the river
When you arrive you are sweaty enough to remove your clothes
You leave them just below the bank
and the water makes them quiver
You give love to who you were and are and will be
The river carries your sweat downstream
Someone else's sweat arrives to swell briefly
around your knees and then it is gone
The origin of the sweat has since left the river far upstream
and they are sweating again
as their car returns them to where they stay
and the riverbed has settled around your feet
and soon its slow current will reveal your toes
You exude the inside out again
Let the river undress

THE ALCHEMIST 2/∞ /AND BEYOND

You write the word "neat" on the rocks
each letter spread across 4 rocks
and you feel that you have done the cleverest thing
until you throw the 4 rocks through your own closed window
making things not-so-neat on the inside

Maybe you should have found 5 more rocks
so you could write "not so" across them
finding then 2 more rocks for the hyphens
which you would then throw through the open window
completing the scene

That is, until you throw an empty scotch bottle
through the empty frame, the bottle shattering
as it lands on a rock labelled "o"

You realize that you are not really so clever
but at least you can dance

You can dance with yourself
or you can dance with someone you love

Or you can hate someone you love
which makes you feel pretty clever

And the person you hate can hate you back
which feels pretty neat

And the person you love can love you back
which is not-so-neat at times
but sometimes it is all you have

There is the Taco Bell where you met the person you love
And the Del Taco where you met the person you hate
And they are on opposite sides of the town

In due time (that is: time that is due to you
for whatever reason) you will both
be floating down the same river

Dogs will swim upstream at quiet intervals
It's always a shock when something happens
that you have been waiting to have happen

(You stick your newly-licked finger into the outlet
of an abandoned house
and when nothing happens
you are shocked
as if you have just seen a ghost)

(We find it impossible to be anything more than gray dots)
(We will wear each other like uniforms)
(We will bear each other's symbols of faith upstream with the dogs)

You think it briefly strange
that you don't pay any attention to the shadows
of others
or they to yours

The river becomes so shallow that you stand up and walk
You feel that your body has grown
The river deepens again and widens

When it is time to climb the waterfall
a fight song plays brightly over the hills
and you choose to let the waterfall beat you into sand

Wait, where is the person you love, you think

It is cool   it is here that you think it cool

The pummeling fight song

Everyone I love has already been pummeled
into shapes too small to identify
but now we can move downstream
as I will move downstream

The quiet of love
The dogs lapping at our faces as we pass

REST

When composers write their symphonies
they don't imagine the 3rd trumpet going home
and releasing dogs into a dark yard
and the mild fear felt
when the dogs disappear from sight

The 3rd trumpet might not view this
as a part of the work
but it is surely a symptom of concern
for when to appropriately destroy the silence

The 3rd trumpet might call out Louis or Winton or say nothing

It is an old house with no exterior lights
The carved-in construction year has been rubbed off the stone by
storm runoff

You patiently await the next phase of your life

When you were eight you wrote postcards to heaven
but you did not stamp them
so they came back to you

You wrote to those who had already arrived:
Abraham Lincoln, Joan of Arc, Harriet Tubman
the trees burned alive in forest fires

the substitute teacher who laughed at your jokes
every dead dog as promised by Disney

A strange man told you Heaven was an all-inclusive resort
so you stopped sending postcards

Water busies itself with digging a river through a forest

It drips future rivers off leaves

There is a browser tab open in the wild
about a recent genocide...
or another cop killing...
or vulture chicks defending their nest...
and then claims to be unresponsive

The weather tab is revealed

It is such a nice beginning to fall

It's like it is still summer
and you can dream of a beach
as if it will manifest
there is a tab for that

In time they will let you realize
that you are really really lost
in your own town

But who doesn't enjoy moving out of an apartment

To walk its emptiness one last time and to find its space
to be smaller than when you first arrived

How I have grown, you might think

You've grown accustomed to how you look
in that specific mirror
in that specific bathroom

You find a cicada shell on your way out
and grind it into your hands like talc

The world has not imagined your departure
It will always be as surprised as you are

Mostly you wanted to be definite
at the cost of the whirligig motion of your fall

To be a statue of rain
Or the opening notes of a music for which you mostly rest

How the faint scratch mark dedication
in the concrete of your porch
is more visible after it rains

How a puddle is a form of communication

How you could maybe lie out in the rain
with your mouth open
and let it fill you

But there is nothing left to say you so often are told

Or you stay inside and hear it layer the roof
and run off into the azaleas

You rest for a while and say nothing

You hear a siren

You say nothing

And when you do it surprises no one but yourself

THE STERILIZATION OF THOUGHT

You sprayed the room the beast was in
and I put it down with The Heart of Prayer
a book given to us with good intentions

!@#$%^&*()_+

It's never easy to understand
why someone would act in any way
until we come to the very idea on our own
at which point the idea feels
as if it has always been a part of us

You can remember being born with the idea

At age right now in your life you think, I should be born
a new beast and so there it is now: your idea

Which explains the way you've always felt about your self

Don't expect to ever forgive your inner beast
That is what others are for, you think
through your new distant thought mechanism
But, most importantly, vice versa

A young forest grows many leaves, casting shadows
It grows old and the leaves fall

You grow old and run through the forest shouting
"Now you see that you must first cast the shadow
before you can see the light"
and you are cold

!@#$%^&*()_+

It will take a beast to remove me
from the heart of my own god
It will first take a bloodhound to find me

I feel glad to not feel
the mosquito bites until much later
when my legs have learned to laugh at them

!@#$%^&*()_+

A new jewel has embedded itself
in the wax of my citronella
which I have burned in the memory
of the most miniscule shadows

There is a new local sports team
and it shares a name with your spirit

The cicadas have surfaced
and they are leaving their shells all over the yard

You forget that you too are human
and must be allowed to have hobbies

You share a feeling or something
with that one group of people from the bible
and I don't know something or a feeling
or something and you try to pin it and label it
like one of those moth beauties you saw at the museum

I forget sometimes that I too
am a radically simplified version
of what I actually think I am

STINKBUG / SAMSUNG

Your body recalls your head
You are hopeless, which means only
that a different kind of light shines from you

A red moth circling the bulb forms a bloody halo
sprouts a pale blossom that withers then grows

The universe regrets nothing it is a dizzy unfolding
It has felt you unfold like a cocktail umbrella in its soup

We stay home and watch the stream
grow coral along the trenches of wifi

At your burial hour
you wear the halo handed down to you
from your mother's father's maker

It flickers like a recurring party thrown
against its own defiance

The dog licks you through its muzzle
which it wears because it cannot control its excitement

You write profane love letters on the fridge

I collect your dead skin cells and pile them
in a weather proof room and watch

as they subtly shift in the A/C wind

When your halo is a constant nuisance
paint the joylight not meant for you

A protagonist so beautiful it is almost you
The idea that the second person is actually the first
That the second is necessary to reach the first unlimited
That the first has disappeared
That when life happens it happens

When I graduated high school I immediately got a job
as a high school graduate - how cool it has been

I wait for you to achieve a new beauty

Twenty seconds pass and there it is

You exaggerate time so beautifully
You are now and then and always

A stinkbug just flew and landed on this line
and then it behaved like a kind drunkard
wandering to the next line up
(the one about now and then and always)
and toppling over and then righting and then flying into your lap
and then into the unlit azalea bush

The congratulations the moment received
was that the sun continued to lower itself

in the field of our perspective
Seeming pauses in a leafless pocket of trees

You have become the stream paused
between the petal and the leaves

We are snow plugs
We wear flurries of powder
We hope to retire where the big bang grew up

Before nothing you were something
but now are spreading across

- — — —·—· --- --—-- - --- -

Now is a cross between never and always
An orchestra set to always

Your chorus triples in size
They kick their heels against the orchestra pit

The tubas sputter and then inform
Enough, they say
You need hear no more

Now we know what to say
Why bother you wonder

Because continue
what is left

THIS HOUSE IS FOR BONE PEOPLE

It is where bones began

You tell me a bone person longs for a skin person
You say hive is just short for high five and you are allergic to high fives
You tell people you have a tattoo that says DEBONE ME

The air is filled with pollen and your body is fighting it
It is acting as if entered by disease

You show me your teen comedy screenplay
In the teen comedy two characters named after us
terrorize the halls of Skin and Bones High
with a flat head screwdriver and our love

The English teacher defeats us by asking us to "deconstruct the atom"
It is not impossible but it takes us the rest of the movie
When the credits begin we take off our tattoos and begin to bone

No it is not like that
You skin me alive
It is like it is real people and not us
I get mopped up by a janitor who has perfected his routine
to the point that he no longer desires vacation

And the sea is married to the sky

A teenager shrieks "YOU ARE MY SAVING GRACE" at another teenager

The student body president petitions
for the water fountains to run with Gatorade

The student body insists

A universe is a song with one verse
A ballad is an advertisement for orbs
A sonnet is a net for catching you, son

The rule of threes is applied directly prior to this line
The rule of twos in this one

And on and on

A funeral home pays the hospital to keep em coming

The light socket filled with the light bone

Because light is the only word
that projects itself from the unlit screen

You have been cast wrong, the doctor whispers
into your brokenness

You are a pretty neat lady, you banter on screen

You will be cast again, explains the fisher to the net

THE LANDLORD'S BIBLE

You total one but it is a big one

Growing up prepared you
for your half-life as a transparency
They shone a light through you
and now the shadow of you hums
against a wall in a school somewhere

They make a wedding dress out of your adolescent poetry
I make a tree fall in the middle of a forest when only we are around

The landlord left a shrink-wrapped bible
in what would've been our junk drawer

We unwrap it together, laughing
We read our favorite verses in sarcastic voices

Our half-lives have been reset

I dedicate my life to your beauty
and all that surrounds you

You cry that you are an as-of-yet
unknown part of the universe

We take turns melting the shrink-wrap onto our eyes
but it makes it impossible to see one another so we peel it off

You compare it to scales or dragonfly wings
I say we have executed so many of god's creatures

We hold the plastic up to the sky
We see the clouds shaking nervously

We each pluck an eyelash off the other
and place them between pages of the landlord's bible
intending to find them before moving out
but we will never find them

They knock on our door
The party on pause
We act like the place is completely empty
which is impossible to do without every eyelash announced

We collapse into our clothes
We undress to greet them
and they too are naked

They immediately shine a light at our chests
that penetrates the skin, exposing our ribcages
which now seem purely decorative

All of this in the doorway leading to the hall

We ask them in and we apologize
for the emptiness of our home
save a bible and some burned cellophane

and our clothes which we would've burned too
if we remembered they were coming

They ask what is your source of fire
and you point to the stove top

We all joke about what we would be doing right now
were the place not empty
save the landlord's bible and some cellophane

The possibilities seem to encounter the expanse
between stars or at least how we could stick thumb tacks
into a closed book as far as our human strength would allow
which is not very far someone decides to the disagreement of a few

Or how we could remove the carpet a fiber at a time

Mostly the talk involves altered states of consciousness
Mostly it is decided that every action is a step toward an altered state

It becomes obvious that we are no longer living the dream
One of us begins dragging the asshole around on the carpet
which makes the place less empty

It is like a tree in a forest with only us around
It is like a tree is a forest with only us around
It is like a tree is a forest in the biblical sense
Or that the other trees are simply transparent

But one of you decides
that a human exhale is the corpse of air
and then one of you counters
that trees are then the eaters of our deaths
though they somehow used the word "expired"
in a way impressive to all of us

We agree we suppose

That nothing is meant forever

One of you suggests
we all should grow out our hair
to the length that it would rip
from our scalps beneath our feet

It won't happen, says a doubter

To let the emergent voices puddle
in the canyons of our skulls
which are purely decorative
someone adds

You are trying to be kind with your life
I am trying to be kind with mine
They are trying to be kind with their lives
I am trying to be kind with mine

You explain crop rotation
and how even the soil must be fed

I describe an experience I had
though it still eludes me

How a piano pushed down a flight of stairs
is preferable to a piano pushed out a second story window

The second story being
the failure of mythology
to explain the adaptation

Or how we know
that the music cannot continue
that the second story
has no direction

ENDURE THE CALM

In the hours before the storm
I imagine the wind through the trees
as a round of applause by the leaves for the leaves
and how the trees stretch and warm up
for the storm now miles behind the wind
I breathe out of my cocoon
flow the rapids of my blood
try to notice whatever mineral structure
has formed in my veins
flow around the tiny obstructions
that may one day stroke me away
to light up my pulse with brine
prepare the fluorescent tomb
that I'll pass through like sediment
or like plankton trapped in the gills
crack shadows like eggs whose yolk
ignites upon the objects of light's obstruction
crack plastic succulents and drink the crude oil
become the storm before the storm preceding storm

OF THIS WORLD

Sometimes it's necessary
to build a bunker in your thoughts
and to climb in with a live one
and to shut the door
and then pull the pin
almost radical
to restart in the middle
of a temporal field somewhere
that gets washed away
and you with it
by like a tidal wave and pummeled
for a while
against the surface of what
counts as what seems
like epiphany
but is really the dumbfoundedness
of believing you have arrived
one step at a time
into the wild part
of reality
or its map unfolded
across the table
of your back

DOGS BARKING

A lesser poet once said
that his luve was like a red, red rose
and then went on to compare his luve
to a song's melody
and he said that his love would endure
all manner of physical and natural tragedy
dry seas, melted rocks, climate change, etc.

My brain is the city in which dogs intermingle
My heart is the suburb in which dogs forever bark
I die in the countryside, found by dogs
for whom barking is a way of song

When we were all done barking
we went up into the universe
and made a baby together: all of us
It wasn't pretty
None of it was pretty
The process
The result
But it happened
and now we're here
and we can't decide upon a name

MICROWAVEOFHEAVEN

In a half-built mansion in the rain
we make a fire out of our clothes
breathing in the thick smoke that billows
from our outer layers
We lie in the sawdust that powders
the unfinished floors
dreaming of moss gowns lichen gowns
forgetting how we arrived
our bodies lapped by the wind flowing
through the opening that would one day usher
guests into a sculpture garden
(We cannot be who we are)
but O the sculpture garden
a Renaissance like wearing plaster
beneath a waterfall
the thrill of being the tallest cop
on the Decapitator
I drop my head into the fountains
eat algae off the black-dappled blue
of what reflects light of night
love you so through the tired of it all
let you into my once in a while
of being draped like a loose fabric
across our spontaneous fire
our smoky moon / our cloudy canopy
in the dance club called "Watching a bug

fulfill its purpose," where I shake free
of bones too heavy
The water marbled with the oil of me
The glistening rubble of my teeth
feeling my speech like atmosphere
I am singing along with the composers of me
before they have had a chance to write the song
In the makeup of who I've become
I smack the universe's ass
It jiggles my hand
and my arm and into my shoulder
I jiggle out of control
My bones snap in the waves
I jiggle in death
against the earth
and into its soil
Roots rumble their way
up the tree to dance on windless days
I reenter being as a log
Stupidly, upon the hill I rest
ready to roll down, collecting bunnies
Where at the bottom I humbly roll
While at the top I dry in sun
Where in the center cooks the center
Where out of lives I take my own
I lodge me safely in the hallway light
where I precede the pilgrimage of moths
whose bodies will burst and embroil with
all that is consumed / made nuclear at last

RIVER ON FIRE

The world usually does not learn your name
and when it does, it's not
for good reasons, which is why
I'm at my lowest when I feel
like I know who I am

When my habits and desires meet
on a burnt out road:
the automatic thought beginning
I feel…
\

\
\

I stream video of burning rivers
smell my body in search of the same chemicals
that let the river catch fire

Toddling through spiderwebs
I become attached to the world
Its reasons for being endure me long
enough for me to endure myself

A prayer against life is a prayer
in which I am paved into the road

skulled in place where forest was shaved
into something useful: a dumpster island
behind a place of 24 hour commerce
and now they really know who I am
and now I really know me as me
now I can endure as a brick: a shadow
of a mountain developed in bursts

A HELL OF TOO MANY MIRACLES

I shoot my dreams out of a cannon
admire their gore as it drips from the fan blades
I walk to the river and into its steadfast
dedication to getting to the point or like
the Liberace quote dangling from the dog's collar:
Too much of a good thing is wonderful
and I disagree with everything ever uttered
I misremember all the moments I've jettisoned
during the mission of being me against so many mes
The kids riding home with skinned knees
brush against the ivy-burdened fence
imagine riding to escape a tyrant
How imagination prepares for the unknown inevitables
of life in a society - any society
but especially this one where everyone is next
I'm told I'm me because I'm born myself
and so I cease to exist when I disown who I am
my traits and my interests all abandoned
and left to sit like a puddle reflecting
what traffic sings above the street
To the burr picked off the sock
and dropped between legs
into the toilet: the ideal life
blossoming in the sewer
I have suffered at the ease
of my existence, I think

and then erase the thought
I leave it up to the Heavens' weight
to crash them through the floor
of whatever receptacle
they've inhabited
since I was born
I give it up to Hell's haunches
that I've developed
and which carry me around

SELF-AWARENESS BRACELET

I try not to give into it
The need to fear
The reluctance to believe
That the leaves will change
with never enough time inside me
I staple my life to its mirror
The staple smiles
I hold my hand up to its reflection
Gift my palm its hidden cool
Who I am smeared like egg into sky
A skeleton adorned with skin
enduring the clunk of heaven's armor
and what it reflects back to its other
and shadows of my own oblivion glued between
I walk forever into dying forests
I walk into myself passing through
Emerge with my bones a mosaic of feeling
I give into the fear
I give into them all
I run rampant through the hallways of anonymity
Shrieking albeits and falsehoods
I shut up against myself and I wither
I wear patches of withering on my skeleton
A graying mosaic now glued with shadow
I urgently perform what I mean
I mean what I am

Deny the paradox of love
Accept only love
Snap off my twig
Dispose of my shoreline
Enact a crusade upon who I am
When I am wartorn really wartorn
I am sacred against God
I am sacred against God
I plant the war in my shadow
and it germinates midsummer
My glue melts
I fall apart
It is not really war
Was never really me
It was my divine failure
I mean no no no
My failure's design
I tell myself it's all just wind in the trees
It's like laughter
And branches fall to impale the earth
And all of this all of this
And a wandering heart dreams of self-duplication
I reach out with all that I span
It's a weird thought I've become

DREAM JOB

My drool sleeps down the pillow and like God chooses not to speak
In my dream, I remove flattened objects: the corpses of sea life
The eye of the dream is fixed as if the dream has been filmed
by a VHS camera mounted on a tripod placed on an uneven surface
I peel the creatures off the rock, which juts out into a cove
on an island somewhere out in the tropics
(It is beautiful, feels profane to even exist here)
and I bring the animals behind what can be seen
as if off screen, the overseer of this task surely resides
reinforcing my completion of the task, giving direction when I slow
I return again and again, peeling these creatures off the rock
not knowing what becomes of their flattened bodies

I know that I am always in this dream, removing the damage
and hiding it from view, reappearing but being sure
that my head always stays above the eye of the dream
as if the eye of the dreamer will discover who I really am

JUMPING INTO A COLD LAKE

You walk through the front doors
of your school
and you and several people
you care deeply about
are promptly
shot
which is fine
because it's actually happened and
now you can stop
dreaming about it

LANDSCAPE IN URGENT CARE

I have kissed the dying part of the world
which is fine
because there will soon be a vaccine for what it carries
and I am already here

You will be here soon

There is a landscape painting hung
next to the window in the examination room
It depicts a dirt path
   forest on the left
      pasture on the right
In the distant part of the pasture
dotted with black cows
in oil paint
I can see you amongst the melting herd
moving steadily this way
I have to believe
you have the cure
and that I am worth saving

SHOWER LIGHTNING

Because I am dirty
I must be made clean

Because I am broken
I must be obscene

Because I am lightning
I must be so frightening

Because I am water
I must be drunk

My dreams that I dream
are closer than ever I thunk

As the water gets hotter
and time freezes over

The dirt I've collected will dance
its way off of my shoulders

        ᚱ   ᚱ   ᚱ   ᚱ   ᚱ   ᚱ

I am selling you a product
It is called Shower Lightning

You will hang the machine in your shower
and you will close your eyes

You will listen to recorded thunder
and imagine yourself naked in a cave

But it doesn't rain in caves, you retort
but caves can have waterfalls too, you dork

The thunder piles in from the mouth of the cave
a wind follows, giving you goosebumps

There is bioluminescence enough to see
the tips of your fingers as they approach the wall

The life forms turn off their light with your approach
but you don't need vision in a cave

The water from the shower hits your face
and your eyes are now closed to see it

The thunder erupts again
and shampoo stings your eyes

You will never be clean
sings the steam from the pipes

Your organs are vital and clean
Your spirit cadavered and splayed

This is what it is to talk and to think, you think
You are the inversion of a miracle, twilighting

The lightning strikes around you but never connects
to the branch on which you're emblazoned

The branch soaked by your memories
like water soaked by the rust of its world

You turn off the shower
allow the storm to continue

You imagine your destruction
the teeth of the vice you maintain

It seems close to you now
The storm sounds so close

But as with destruction there is a dial
to create the illusion of distance and safety

It is measured in miles
and your fingers can move the storm away

You can make it seem safe
You can even turn it off

Really, you don't even need Shower Lightning
but the truth is that you want it

I find it impossible to lie to you
I am the future of marketing

It is a matter of desire and not of necessity
that the storm surrounds and negates your sense of comfort

It is a matter of your own internal clutter
that you have not already noticed the eruption

Now open your windows
Let the branches breathe their way in

FUTURE CONVERSATIONS BETWEEN TWO TREES AND SOME OTHER THINGS TOO

Once all the humans are gone
the remaining living creatures will converse
like...
One tree says to another, "What are you up to?"
And the second tree says, "Just trying to get sober"
And the first tree says, "Yeah, me too"
And the second says, "Sucks, don't it?"
And the first says, "Oh yeah. My bark itches"
And the second says, "What?"
And the first says, "My bark itches"
And the second says, "Oh ok. For some reason
I started thinking about dogs when you said bark"
And the conversation goes on like this until one
or both trees tire of talking

The humans will be gone
The dull of the earth will be noticableble
to whatever might be floating around in space
in view of the earth, planet of former empires
whose cities' illumination
built upon violence
used to be
a feature like the deep dark bioluminescence
of the ocean

The deep dark of the ocean
will look to the deep dark of space
and think, Ah, stars again
And the deep dark of space
will look to the deep dark of the ocean
and think, Ah
And the in between will be steady
with cities overgrown
and highways uprooted
and prisons made thick with vines
and reservoirs shallowed
and satellites straying
and only the light of the sun
and the rivers still vomiting
the awful they've swallowed
into seas for whom vomit
is merely a meal
for the dark parts
whose light parts
are no longer light

Most poem to movie adaptations
would now have the part where
the last human emerges fist first from a glacier
only to stumble with final effort onto a rock where he dies
And most movies would have him wake up
but in this one our hero remains dead
and the trees continue to sober up
and the river continues to vomit

beneath the satellites on journeys
to crash into planets
after not enough time
spent spinning through space
and the waves all now trash
the shores of the cities
leaving wilderness coastlines
all rocky like cities now buried by forests
whose trees are now filled with the breath
of what still moves

And the trees after resting become ready to talk
The first one says, "I feel like I can hear again"
The second says, "What?"
The first sighs
"No, I'm kidding," says the second
"I know what you mean," even though
the second tree has no idea

CHRISTIAN MANGLE

Impaled on my brain
is the hat hook on which I hang
many haloes, those of my idiocy
and of the people I enjoy
the voices of improbability
steaming on the hook
like a wet sun

When someone says ha
this is the h in christ
the stigmata that ingests
the hurt of the world
in which all the people
in my phone
simultaneously laugh
a non-prescription laugh
that is unhearable
but bright

INEVITABILITIES

We allow the water to lick the plate clean
of its grease and its gunk
and we allow not time but tiny beings
to clean the skin from our bones

On a Sunday I am wounded
by the television
I use my hair as a tourniquet
and my other skin as a bandage

I have to learn a new heartbeat
if I'm to live in the future
string a tightrope between myself
and each person I know
fall into the chasms between us
and incubate
glide a warship silently into oblivion

They'll write books about it
and in the books I wash dishes
at the bank of a river
and I leave the dishes in the river as rocks
and I turn off the river
and darken the sky
and I say, "I'll tell a story
and then another story

but not today
and maybe not tomorrow"
and I put away the scenery
and I exit the scene

THE EVAPORATOR

Suppose that I died
by crashing my car into a telephone pole
on my way into the City of Leaves
but upon my moment of death
my life simply continued
And now you sit here
with these words that do not exist
And yet all seasons simultaneously greet you
Leaves fall into your lap
while wild tulips emerge
from the soil of living
The visitors have arrived at your garden
They take pictures
I have felt this before
My body has produced waste
I have asked the river
where it is going
The visitors note that the river
does not photograph well
The atoms cease to move once captured
The park ranger winks at me
before describing "the light of my spirit"
They comment on the light
and its dutiful treatment of things
I owe a handstand to the weeds
and a somersault to the subtle valley

And if I'm dead then why am I
still paying for things
This is a public park
and my wallet is making it
hard to walk
I throw my wallet into the river and forget
And if I had not died
would we have met?
When I arrived in the City of Leaves
they were not surprised at my arrival
They pointed to the trail
and told me to enjoy the day
And I did enjoy the day
but enjoyment always rubs against
the worry that we've purchased from the living
The trail was wet from the morning's rain
with puddles slowly evaporating
I laid down next to a puddle
and I challenged it to a race upward
Last to the sky is a rotten egg, I said
and we began
and every part of me is still lying there
in anticipation of ascension
BTW, the puddle always wins
always returns but never remembers
to call me a rotten egg
When the visitors ask what I'm doing
I remind them that this is public land
and I'm not breaking any laws

They take my photograph (sometimes with puddle
sometimes without) and walk on
The daytime relaxes
I move a few decimals
I mouth voila to the sky
I relieve beauty's burden
I should not have waited this long
to compose my will
There is nothing left of me
And the only specialist who accepts
my insurance is a lepidopterist
But what do I know?
I know that if you crawled inside of me
you would find a forest cleaved
by a slow river
I know that chrysalis is the most
stressful time of year
I know you will be here soon

WORRY STONE

I come up with a better word for the world
and I speak it directly into the earth's air
I drink cold water from an insulated cup

The earth is untidy
Catkins cover every artificial surface
attempting to inseminate the plastic's flower

In the previous time zone
it is happy hour
In our time zone
the weeping will soon cease

I have climbed a tall tree
and have written a different word for love
on each leaf
In the fall I will know how to say
what I already know how to say

I breathe oxygen from a ficus in Columbia
A meteorite wound geysers oil
which we will use to anoint the seasons with light
I keep a shard of the meteorite
in my pocket as a worry stone
By the time I finish my thought
it will be rubbed smooth

My thumb will be calloused
but that is good, yes

I must say it is good now and then
I must say, "O yes, I love water"
as I drink again from my cup
I must view it as my duty to say it
I hope to always mean what I say
and for what I say to enhance the image
of the world that I see
and love
but remember that even love's puddle
reflects what is above it
and below it
and that even a puddle
has a shadow
and all of these things
flourish in thought

I WAS A SWAMP

In a previous life, I was a swamp
and now in this life driving into a large city
feels like driving into the internet
I wish I had enough money to buy every billboard
between my house and the opposite side of the large city
In every billboard a picture of family
Family, in this case, being different swamps
Each swamp emitting a glitch cloud of gnats
Each inch of interstate a little heavier than before
despite its wear beneath the commuter tires

In the morning, I log into who I am
feeling like the real thing
I drive seven minutes to the school where I work
I cross the swollen river
Drive parallel to my city's loop
Swipe a card to enter the building
Enter my numbers into the machine

Throughout the day, we talk about ways
to become better people
I try to settle into who I am at any given moment
I am honest about who I am, a former swamp
I sat inside myself so long that I dried up and a meadow replaced me
No one protected me
There is something there, I tell my students, if you look

A flip phone buried in the dirt - once the mud of me
Lost by a naturalist observing mating fireflies
My leftover spirit suckling through the wires, attempting to speak
I say all of us have our swamps or deserts or taigas
that will one day consume us
We grow up within them
Everything about us forms the breadth of the myth
of human nature
of atomic being

I drive home to my neighborhood cut into the woods above the river
turn off who I am as I hide from the world
bathed in the red of a new episode
consumed by the glow of my bedside clock
each digit a firefly mating across the dry skin of my face

How waking up thirsty I know I've lived better lives

But who I am at any moment is who I am at any moment
And who you are at any moment is who you are at any moment

And tomorrow I will forget what I've learned
I will point my phone's camera into a puddle to collect my reflection
I will send my reflection into the wild of digitalia
where, at any moment, we are all who we are
Or at least we are the billboards of who we hope to be
standing on the edge of the city, ready
to jump off its edge and into its dirt packed hard
into the crystal that reflects its underside

A spiritual crime scene in which all criminals are free to go
We must coax them into who they are at any moment given
They, the names of complex systems of being in which
everything is of use, then respond by committing crimes against perpetuity
Dissolving infinities in unchristened sewers
We merely fit into the way of things
Read into our harm as if a scar is not merely the universe's way
of autographing our bodies

My biggest spiritual crime as a swamp was letting myself dry up
How so much of me went up into the clouds
and followed the wind to the next thing
How unlike a god I am
How I wish to stand above myself with a watering can
and drink of who I used to be: a thing
that believed instead of a thing
to which doubt and belief are the same

My second biggest spiritual crime was not becoming a fountain
that churns the pools of everyone else, chlorinated and bright
whose lessons are learned in the acceptance of what fills it
and whose coins will tarnish amid the rivers of commerce

I am a swamp
I am a swamp
I am a swamp
This is my attempt
to regain my form

My third and final spiritual crime
is attempting to be anything
other than what I am
A transfer of atoms from now to now
I will be executed by all who love me
in the gentlest way possible
They will rain into me
and I will grow into a perverse thing
I will disperse
I will have no shadow
I will only accept the sun
I will grow into a cloud of memory
I will find a plot of sky and keep moving

THE SUPER BOWL OF SELF CARE

1

We called it an "earth-shattering"
We brought hammers and axes
and every manner of destruction
Guns and cannons pointed downward
We dropped cars from cranes
Pushed mountains off of mountains
Spiked volcanoes with sugar and gunpowder

The earth maintained

This is stupid, someone said
It's mind-blowingly stupid

That gives me an idea, someone else said

Instead of an earth-shattering
let's do a mind-blowing

And everyone enjoyed that
We took turns
blowing one another's minds
It got messy but the scenery adjusted
It smelled lotion into faultlines, industrialized solitude
stitched faces into halo shapes

The halo became obsolete
This is good, thought the thoughts
The earth would not shatter
but the mind could be blown
Like a candle
Like a tire
Like a scene from a teen movie

And now
I get high, salute manhood
My mind is still blown
I throw it all against a cloud
The world's mind is still blown
It hangs like a halo on a coat rack
drips down the spine of night and day
The world's mind
The earth's retina leaking like yolk

Oh, how shattering

And everyone takes it up
into their senses
We dig our fingers into earth
I tell myself
(the world bends you)
(bend it back)
but I know
(I am here now)
(I evade heaven on a tightrope)
and I forget myself

So we shatter or hope to
shatter what is left of the earth: all of it
Every continent. Every ocean
Even the dirt upon which we slam
clouds apart like unvacuumed prayer rugs
We believe ourselves strong
I believe myself strong
I have fought and vanquished millions
on a cliff's edge, dusted them off into the ravine
Yet when I kick through it
I dust nothing, break nothing, blow nothing
cake dirt on my clothes and then vomit
in the heat, explore the beefy mystery
of our self-guided cataclysm
our wintering sun

2

Off the shore somewhere a plastic galleon anchors
Its crew sprays aerosol bible verses onto the crust of the waves

> When you find a hole in the earth, thrust your fist
> fearlessly into it

> In the presence of mystery, prevent revelation

> Or be the contradiction you wish to see in the world
> Let clarity of thought obscure what surrounds you

> A god violently shaking a person-shaped abacus

> Or a child shaking a god-shaped abacus

Two giant, broken robots float through space
One says, We are flotsam and jetsam
They twist at a slow rate
They look into the distance in search of planets to scour for fuel
The second robot says who is which
The first one says, I'm jetsam
And tries to activate his palm jet
Our lives ignite upon the shores of here and there
And our existence depends upon it
Exists against us
A tomb filled with disgraced emperors flows through
the vein of our own personal cosmos

Rocks break against the waves for once
Wait upon the waves for once
Another space at once

How the sun and rain sustain
without question
The flora emancipated the fauna
Loaded words guide themselves
like missiles into the clouds
The unsustainable sun and FMLA
The weight of an acorn vs. the storm
Walking into hell as who I've always been
and walking out as who I could never
And purchasing monarch butterflies and growing them inside
the hollow part of the cloud or the unclaimed chambers of myself
de-winged upon the profane altar of now
The atoms shaped like everyone attacking
the atoms shaped like everyone else

In joy, I am worthless
In purchase, I am a known entity
I worked hard for the soil of my body
to become this hospitable
I will work even harder to become
a beautiful garden into which
our dying star can be interred

3

The mountain climbs itself
and offshore
the galleon is gutted by the reef
The water cripples the shore
The shore is torn open
Who is in there but you and I
in civil combat
The water fills what has been
ripped of the shore
The wreckage continues upon us
The mountaintop grinds into sky

We howl through the top of the water
Classic rock, we pray against the surface
Let us be a skipped sea shell too light for the task
swallowed by the breast of the wave

Oh, my cloud evorapating
I chug the cloud while I can
Someone says, can I waterfall off of that
and I say, what? They say, nevermind
but they steal my juice anyway
It is regular time. It is just a season
The water and the air have temperatures
One must read them to know the temperatures
Lord knows the clouds

And robots grow ever knowing
We must know them as they know us
Our tantrums obvious against those we know as us
too empowered to even be real among the other
I hail into the city above which I shadow
I give hail to the canopy that shadows all below me
I've been baptized in leaves
Lord help me
I've been baptized enough to know
that the spirit evaporates
I am air-dried and ready
to fall again

4

And now on the Wednesday night of this afternoon
up the river that dumps into the ocean
I am here
I just sit and think
Me and the old men who might also be me
though they look nothing like me
listen to the muddy churn
become disoriented by the contrast
of the swift current
to the line of the shore
We attract flies with our decay
our bodies and minds so poisoned into the need
to sit by the river and think
100 yards downshore from one another
All of us beautiful gardens
future hosts of dying suns

And everything downstream will feel this later
I affix my gaze or I stumble upon a molecule
of water that has yet to be there
in its prime
But then again it is water's supposed purity
that we hope to embody
Or the futility of it
this crashing through space
or of denying the mosquito it's taste

And as the singer dangles
from the moon so dangles
the song from the self
Amplified for all and walloped into interpretation
And interpretation given chuckles
the show itself not its self
but what I mean to myself
A language as a starter pack to understanding
sung unintelligibly, blasted into everyone
Everyone shrieks out their stigmata
A fecal solar system in short blasts
The spirit evaporates on Fridays
falls back to earth on Monday
when it must endure the ambitions of others
Society daydreams upon us
We wake up inside the daydream not ourselves
not in love but of the fleshy lousing of living
what we wish to exist within and not upon
But in the daydream we are worked upon, given nightmares
We are the fear of the other: humanity's
headwound sunk with cleats
The song ends; the singer still dangles
The game ends in order
that we look to the next one
arranged into Purinas of ascension
and the wonder of being here
in the ill-fitting future with everything to heal
a blown mind, a shattered earth, the repetition of us

ACKNOWLEDGEMENTS

Thank you to Elizabeth for your kind eye and wonder.

"The Lightning Rod of Everything," "The Waterfallness of the Water," and "The Alchemist 2/∞/Beyond" originally appeared in *NY Tyrant*.

"Tonight You Will Love a River" and "We Begin by Exploding" appeared in *gesture*.

"Dogs Barking," "Christian Mangle," "Shower Lightning," "Inevitabilities," and "I Was a Swamp" originally appeared in *Gay Death Trance*.

"Joy Your Heart Against Me" originally appeared in *The Mantle*.

"Monument" and "You Light the Citronella" originally appeared in *Hobart*.

"Endure the Calm" and "River on Fire" originally appeared *Always Crashing*.

"Self-Awareness Bracelet" and "Worry Stone" originally appeared in *Screaming into a Horse's Mouth*.

"The Evaporator" originally appeared *Neutral Spaces'* Birthday Magazine.

"The Super Bowl of Self Care" originally appeared in *HAD*.